JNF
629.45
Fur
Furniss, Tim
The first men on the moon

THE FIRST MEN ON THE MOON

Tim Furniss

Illustrated by Peter Bull

The Bookwright Press
New York · 1989

Great Journeys

The First Men on the Moon
The Travels of Marco Polo
The Voyage of the Beagle
The Race to the South Pole

Further titles are in preparation

First published in the
United States in 1989 by
The Bookwright Press
387 Park Avenue South
New York, NY 10016

First published in 1988 by
Wayland (Publishers) Limited
61 Western Road, Hove
East Sussex BN3 1JD, England

© Copyright 1988 Wayland (Publishers) Limited

Library of Congress Cataloging-in-Publication Data
Furniss, Tim.
　The first men on the moon.

　(Great journeys)
　Bibliography: p.
　Includes index.
　Summary: Describes the development of the Apollo spacecraft which succeeded in landing men on the moon in 1969.
　1. Project Apollo—Juvenile literature. 2. Space flight to the moon—Juvenile literature. [1. Project Apollo. 2. Space flight to the moon] I. Title. II. Series.
　TL789.8.U6A5354 1989　629.45'4
88-24166
　ISBN 0-531-18240-1

Typeset by DP Press Ltd, Sevenoaks, Kent
Printed in Italy by G. Canale & C.S.p.A., Turin

Cover *Neil Armstrong and Edwin "Buzz" Aldrin landed on the moon on July 20, 1969. They were the first men to set foot on the lunar surface.*

Frontispiece *This footprint was left on the moon by one of the Apollo 11 astronauts.*

Contents

1. The Race to the Moon — 4
2. The Apollo 11 Astronauts — 6
3. Training for Space — 8
4. The Saturn 5 Rocket — 10
5. The Spacecraft — 12
6. The Spacesuits — 14
7. The Launch — 16
8. From the Earth to the Moon — 18
9. Eagle Lands on the Moon — 20
10. Walking on the Moon — 22
11. Homeward Bound — 24
12. Splashdown — 26
13. The Legacy of Apollo 11 — 28

Glossary — 30
Finding Out More — 31
Index — 32

The Race to the Moon

Early in the twentieth century the dream of leaving earth for space and flying to the moon began to look as if it might come true. By the 1930s engineers in the USSR and the United States had managed to develop small liquid-fueled rockets. A breakthrough came in World War II when Germany shocked the world with the large V2 rockets, which were used to bombard Britain. At the end of the war, some German V2 engineers went to the USSR and others went to to the United States. So the basic rockets that had already been developed in these countries were improved by new ideas from the V2 teams.

In 1956 the United States announced plans to launch into orbit the first earth satellite, using the Vanguard rocket. The Russians replied that they too would launch a satellite, and

Below *This diagram shows the journey of Apollo 11. If you follow the arrows carefully you can work out all the different stages of the mission. The photograph (inset below) shows Apollo 11 just after its takeoff.*

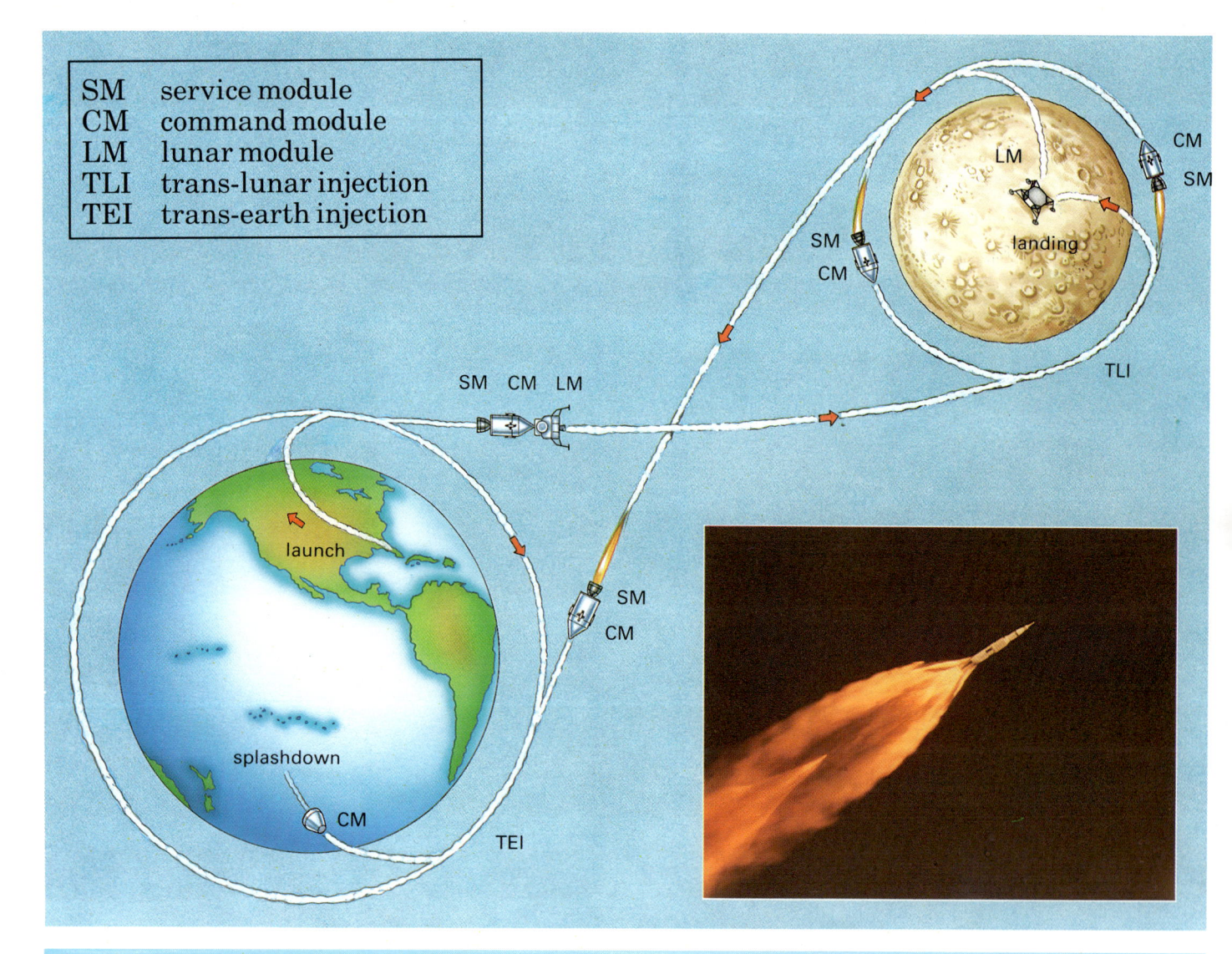

SM   service module
CM   command module
LM   lunar module
TLI   trans-lunar injection
TEI   trans-earth injection

Right *Yuri Gagarin of the USSR became the first man in space when he flew in the Vostok 1 spacecraft in April 1961. Two years later, in June 1963, Valentina Tereshkova of the USSR became the first woman in space when she traveled in the Vostok 6 spacecraft. They were both given many medals and awards for these journeys.*

even said how big it would be. Nobody took any notice, because they expected the Americans to launch first. But on October 4, 1957, the Russians launched their satellite.

Sputnik 1 surprised the United States. It was very heavy, weighing over 80 kg (176 lb). The United States did not own such a powerful rocket. To make matters worse, a tiny United States satellite, Vangard TV-3, was destroyed in an explosion on its launch pad the following December. This embarrassing failure was called "Flopnik" and "Kaputnik" by the press.

The United States continued to be beaten to its target by the USSR. Russian spacecrafts were the first to reach the moon and to photograph its hidden far side in 1959. Then, as the first of seven astronauts chosen for the American Mercury program was preparing to be sent into space, on April 12, 1961, the Russians did it again. They launched cosmonaut Yuri Gagarin as the world's first space traveler. United States President John F. Kennedy needed something to improve his nation's pride in its space program, and on 25 May, 1961, he announced that the United States would land a man on the moon before 1970. Assuming that the USSR was also in a "race" to the moon, the goal was to get there as quickly as possible.

The project to put Americans on the moon was called the Apollo program. Its aims were these: an enormous rocket, the Saturn 5, would launch the Apollo spacecraft (containing command, service and lunar modules) toward the moon. The astronauts on this spacecraft would be the first men to land and walk on the moon.

The Apollo 11 Astronauts

The Apollo program reached its climax with the launch of Apollo 11, the spacecraft that was to carry a crew of three astronauts to a landing on the moon. The crew members were not chosen because they were the greatest American test pilots or astronauts; in fact, their final selection for the mission was a matter of sheer luck. In January 1969, astronauts Neil Armstrong, Buzz Aldrin and Michael Collins found themselves next on the list to fly a space mission.

Neil Alden Armstrong, commander of Apollo 11, was born in Wapakoneta, Ohio, on August 5, 1930. He had soloed in an airplane before he could drive a car! Armstrong joined the Navy as a twenty-year-old and flew 78 combat missions during the Korean War. Armstrong later became a civilian test pilot at Edwards Air Force Base in California. There he flew what was considered by pilots to be the ultimate flying machine – the X-15 rocket plane. One of his seven X-15 missions took him up to a height of over 60 km (37 mi). In September 1962 Armstrong became an astronaut with the

Above *The Apollo 11 crew consisted of (from left to right) Neil Armstrong, Michael Collins and Edwin "Buzz" Aldrin.*

National Aeronautics and Space Administration (NASA), along with eight other test pilots, and began training for the Gemini program. Gemini was a two-man spacecraft designed to fly in the earth's orbit. Its job was to test all the skills and movements required for the planned moon flight, including the rendezvous and docking. As commander of Gemini 8, in March 1966 Armstrong became the first man to dock two spacecraft together.

The Apollo astronauts shared many similar characteristics. They were pilots of proven skill, old enough to have good service records, calm and reliable under pressure, and with steady family backgrounds.

Chosen as command module pilot of the Apollo 11 mission was Michael Collins. He would be required to remain alone in lunar orbit while Armstrong and Aldrin made their descent and moon landing. Collins was born in Rome, Italy, on October 31, 1930. He too became an Air Force test pilot at Edwards Air Force Base and was selected for the third NASA astronaut group with Aldrin and twelve others in October 1963. Collins's first space mission was on the Gemini 10 flight in July 1966, when he walked in space. Collins was chosen to fly on the Apollo 8 mission, which made ten orbits of the moon in December 1968, but had to withdraw to have an operation.

The pilot of Apollo 11's lunar module was Edwin "Buzz" Aldrin. He had the job of monitoring all the spacecraft controls while Armstrong managed the landing. Aldrin was to have been first to set foot on the moon until Armstrong decided during training that, as commander, he would take the responsibility of stepping out first.

Aldrin was born in Montclair, New Jersey, on January 30, 1930. He joined the U.S. Air Force and flew 66 combat missions in Korea. After his selection as an astronaut in October 1963, he piloted Gemini 12 in November 1966. Aldrin spent a record total of 5 hours 37 minutes outside the spacecraft.

Above When they were training, the astronauts acted out many of the tasks that they would have to do on the moon.

Below Armstrong and Aldrin fought in the Korean War. Their duties as pilots helped the astronauts to train for their space mission.

Training for Space

The Apollo 11 mission lasted eight days, or about 200 hours. For every one of those hours in flight, each crew member had spent five hours of formal training for the actual mission. Each astronaut had also made one Gemini spaceflight, gaining practical training for the mission.

Apollo 11 training consisted of lectures, as well as practical training and experience in machines that simulated, or copied, conditions to be expected in space and spaceflight. There were talks on spacecraft systems, to learn how all the controls worked, and more than 400 hours of training for each astronaut in command module and lunar module simulators. Simulations of launch and re-entry into the earth's atmosphere took place in a spinning centrifuge. There were also simulations of every activity to be performed on the moon's surface.

The astronauts all practiced working in the weightless conditions they would experience once Apollo left earth's gravity. This "weightlessness" was achieved inside aircraft flying special curved paths, and also in an underwater tank.

Below *The astronauts trained underwater to learn how to move around in weightless conditions. This diver is taking photographs of an astronaut underwater so that scientists can study his movements.*

For most of the flight the crew members were to wear light overalls; these were strong enough for floating around in the command module and the lunar module ascent stage. There was not much room and it got smelly too; the craft was not just a living room but the bathroom, toilet and kitchen as well. Most of the crew's food was dried and had to have water added to it. A typical menu would be fruit cocktail, sausage patties, cocoa, flavored bread cubes and a grapefruit drink. The astronauts brushed their teeth using normal toothpaste but had to use "wet wipes" since there was no running water for washing. They urinated using a special container. The urine was then thrown into space. Feces were collected in plastic bags. The bags were sealed and stored for inspection by doctors after the return to earth. Astronauts wearing spacesuits could urinate into a special container in the suit leg; to excrete feces they wore special underwear (although fortunately none had to use it for this purpose).

The crew had an emergency medical kit. There were no suicide pills. If a problem should prevent the astronauts from returning to earth, they were to continue to work and send messages to the earth for as long as they could. In case they landed back on earth a long way from their target, the crew took survival gear including a life-raft, water, knapsacks and knives.

Below *When a plane dives in steep curves, it creates an occasionally weightless condition, which is similar to that found in space. The astronauts used these flights to practice moving around in weightless conditions.*

The Saturn 5 Rocket

The Saturn 5 booster was developed for the sole purpose of sending astronauts to the moon. It was the most powerful rocket in the world until 1987 when the Russian Energia booster was produced. The Saturn 5 made its first test flight in November 1967, stunning observers at the Kennedy Space Center with its power and noise, which shook buildings several miles away. Everything about the rocket was enormous (see table).

The first stage had five F-1 engines, which each second gulped more than 8,000 liters (2,000 gal) of propellants. The center engine was fixed but the outer four could be swiveled to help steer the booster. Liftoff is called T by space scientists. At T plus 2 minutes 15 seconds the center engine shut down. The other four engines shut down 25 seconds later, and the first stage fell away. By this time, the Saturn 5 rocket had risen 67,000 m (220,000 ft) and was traveling at over 2,700 m

Below and far right
The Saturn 5 was a very large and powerful rocket. The astronauts had to use an elevator to reach the spacecraft on top of it.

Saturn 5 Statistics (approximate)

Total height	110 m (360 ft)
Total weight	2,800 tons
Total engine thrust	4 million kg (8.8 million lb)
First Stage	
Height	42 m (138 ft)
Width	10 m (33 ft)
Thrust	3.5 million kg (7.6 million lb)
Second Stage	
Height	24 m (80 ft)
Width	10 m (33 ft)
Thrust	500,000 kg (1.1 million lb)
Third Stage	
Height	17.6 m (58 ft)
Width	6.7 m (22 ft)
Thrust	104,000 kg (230,000 lb)
Command Module	
Height	3.5 m (11.5 ft)
Base diameter	4 m (13 ft)
Weight	6 tons

(8,800 ft) per second.

Three seconds after separation, the five engines of the Saturn's second stage ignited, producing a thrust of some half a million kg (1.1 million lb). The second-stage engines burned liquid oxygen and liquid hydrogen fuel. As with the first stage, the four outer engines burned for longer than the center engine. When they shut down, 9 minutes and 10 seconds into the flight, the Saturn was about 186 km (116 mi) above the earth and traveling at 7,000 m (23,000 ft) per second. After the final shutdown, the second stage separated exposing the single engine of the third stage.

The third stage called the S4B, had first to place Apollo into a "parking orbit" around the earth. Its second task was to start up again to send the craft toward the moon. The S4B burned more than 100 tons of liquid hydrogen and liquid oxygen. Eleven minutes and forty seconds after launch, traveling at over 7,700 m (25,000 ft) per second, the engine shut down and the S4B and Apollo entered earth's orbit together. Nestled within the top of the S4B was the Apollo lunar module.

Another extremely important component of the Saturn rocket was the Instrument Measuring Unit, which helped to steer it. It contained guidance, navigation and control systems. This unit also contained communications, crew safety, and electrical systems.

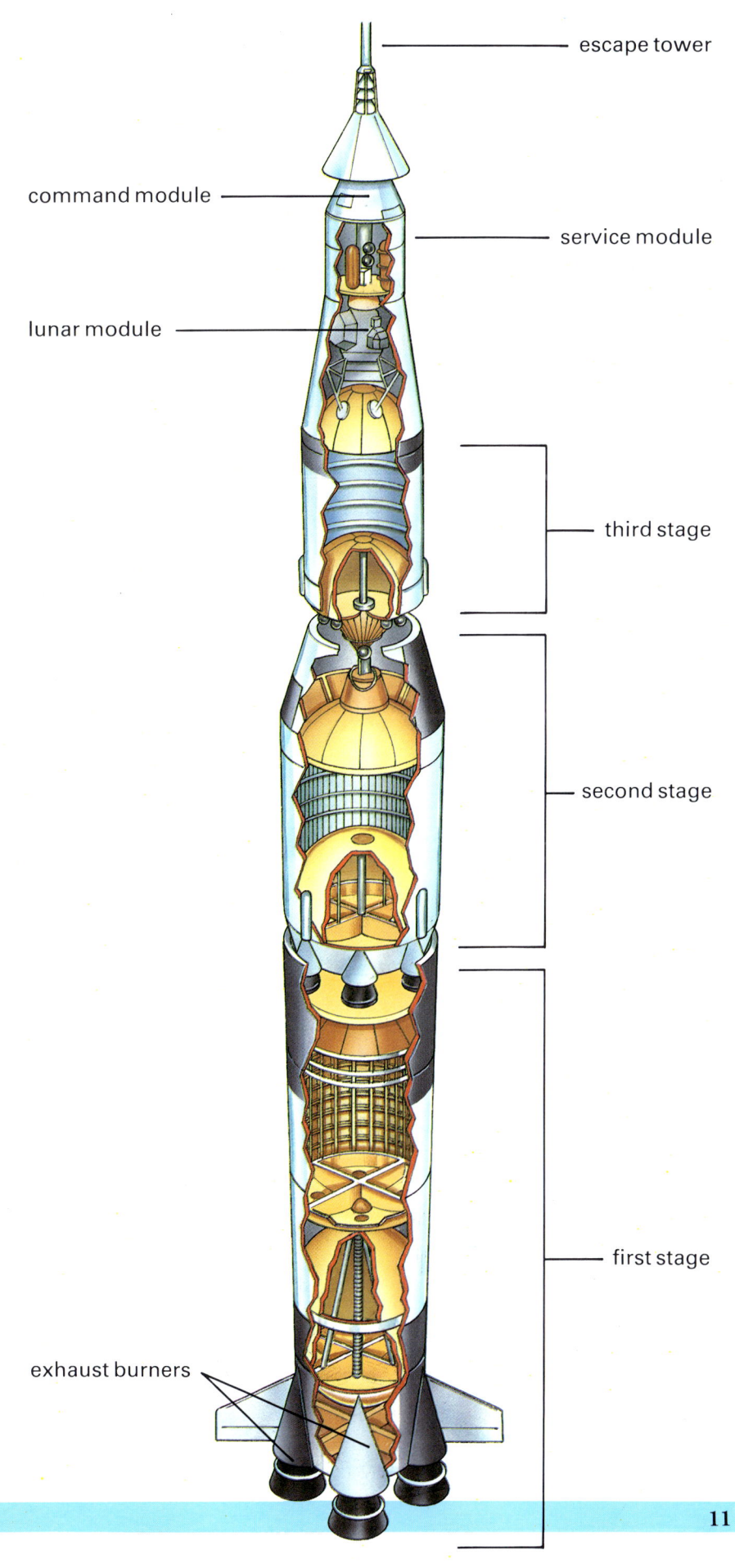

The Spacecraft

Left *The astronauts lay in the command module on couches placed very close together. This picture, which shows the couches with only one astronaut in position, demonstrates how little room there was in the module.*

The Apollo craft was in three parts, or modules: a combined command and service module and a lunar module. At the time, the Apollo craft were the most sophisticated and highly technical spacecraft ever built.

On top of the Saturn 5 launcher was a launch escape system. This was a rocket 10 m (33 ft) high designed to pull the command module away from the main booster if anything went wrong with the launch. If everything went normally, the launch escape system rocket was ejected during the second stage of the launch. As it was ejected, it pulled away a cover that protected the whole of the command module. So, for the early phase of the launch, the astronauts inside the command module were "blind" because their windows were covered.

The cone-shaped command module was home for the three men for most of the eight-day moon mission. Its most important part was probably the heat shield. When the command module came back to earth it would be traveling at 40,000 kph (25,000 mph). Hitting the earth's atmosphere at such high speed would create extraordinary friction, which would generate heat capable of burning the spacecraft to ashes within seconds. The heatshield was designed to prevent this. It was a stainless steel honeycomb structure, covered with an outer layer of special resin. Stowed at the top of the command module were three large parachutes, which would open to slow the craft for a final soft splashdown.

Beneath the command module was the service module. Over 7 m (23 ft) long, it contained the essential systems needed to maintain the flight of the command module. These included fuel cells that generated electricity. The service module also had an engine that would be fired to send the spacecraft into lunar orbit.

For the flight from the earth to the moon, the lunar module had to be removed from its launch position on top of the third stage of the Saturn 5 vehicle and be attached to the front end of the command module. The lunar module was 7 m (23 ft) high and about 9.5 m (30 ft) wide. It was covered with thin layers of foil to protect it from heat and damage from being hit by tiny meteorites. It had two halves: an ascent stage and a descent stage. The ascent stage accommodated the two astronauts who would fly down to land on the moon. Its cabin was about 3.5 m (11 ft) high and 4 m (13 ft) wide. It was also equipped with an engine to lift off from the moon, using the descent stage as a launch pad. If the engine did not fire, the astronauts would be doomed to stay forever on the moon. The descent stage too had an engine; it would fire to reduce the speed of the lunar module as it came in to land. It had four landing legs, each with a large footpad. The astronauts would use a ladder on one of the legs to descend to the moon. After exploring the moon, the descent stage would be left on the surface.

Below *This illustration shows the command module and service module of the Apollo 11 spacecraft and the Saturn 5 rocket.*

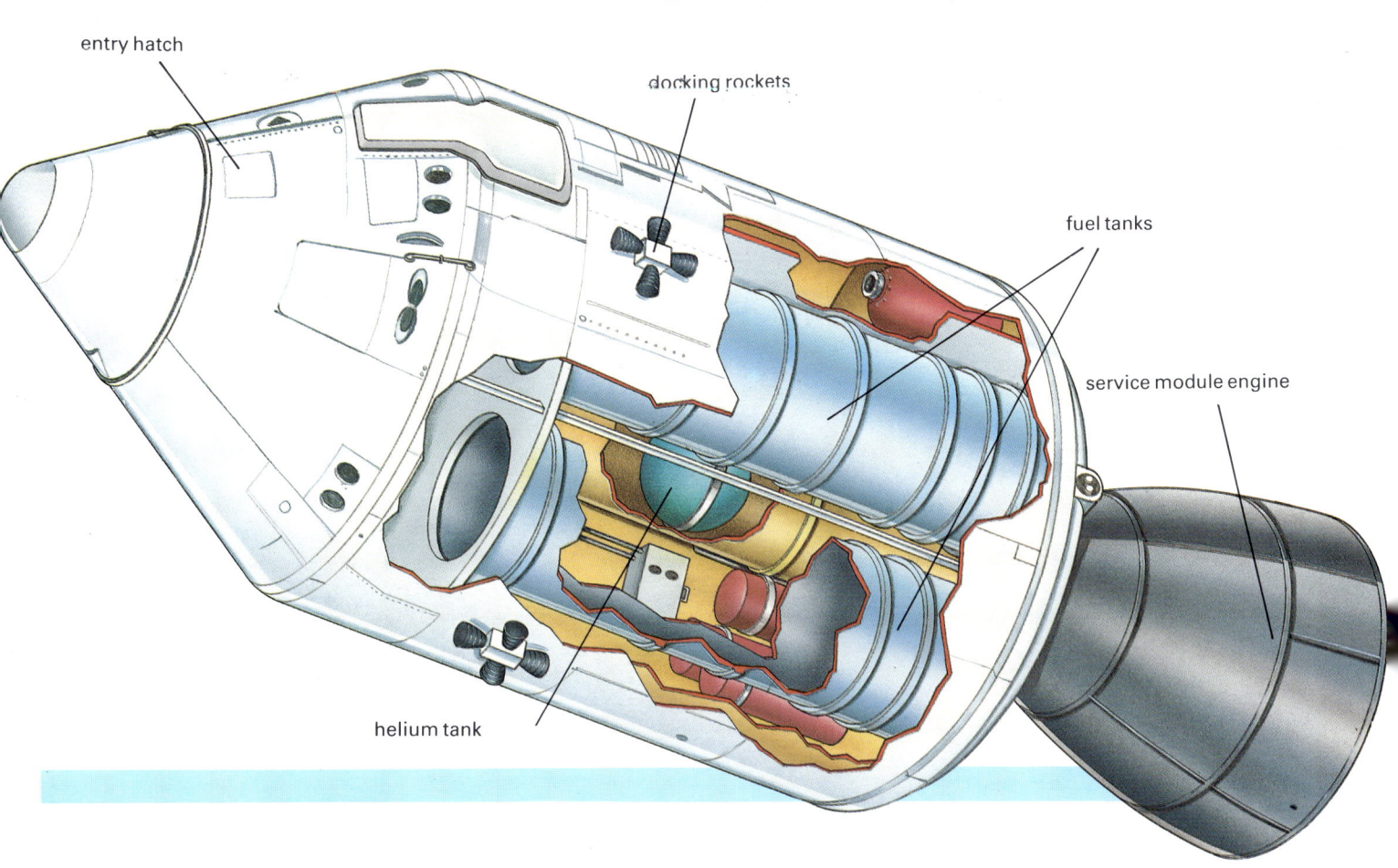

The Spacesuits

During critical parts of Apollo flights (such as launch, engine firings and reentry), the crew wore spacesuits to protect them in case there was a loss of cabin pressure. When walking on the moon, astronauts needed extra protection against intense heat and cold, radiation and possible meteorite impact. So there were two versions of the Apollo spacesuit. One was a pressure suit worn by the command module pilot (who remained in orbit above the moon). The other was the Extra Vehicular Activity, or EVA, pressure suit worn for the moonwalks. The suits were similar, except that the EVA suit had an extra layer for added protection.

The basic suit consisted of many layers of man-made and coated cloths. It had gloves and a large "goldfish bowl" helmet. The astronauts wore soft "Snoopy hats" under the helmet, which had built-in microphones and earphones for radio contact with earth. Beneath the suit the astronaut wore zippered "long john" underwear. The total suit

Right *This illustration shows the many layers of the spacesuits. The ribbed layer was underwear that was filled with water to keep the astronaut cool.*

Below *Many people were needed to help the astronauts put on their heavy spacesuits. The photograph on the right shows clearly the "Snoopy hats" that they wore under their helmets.*

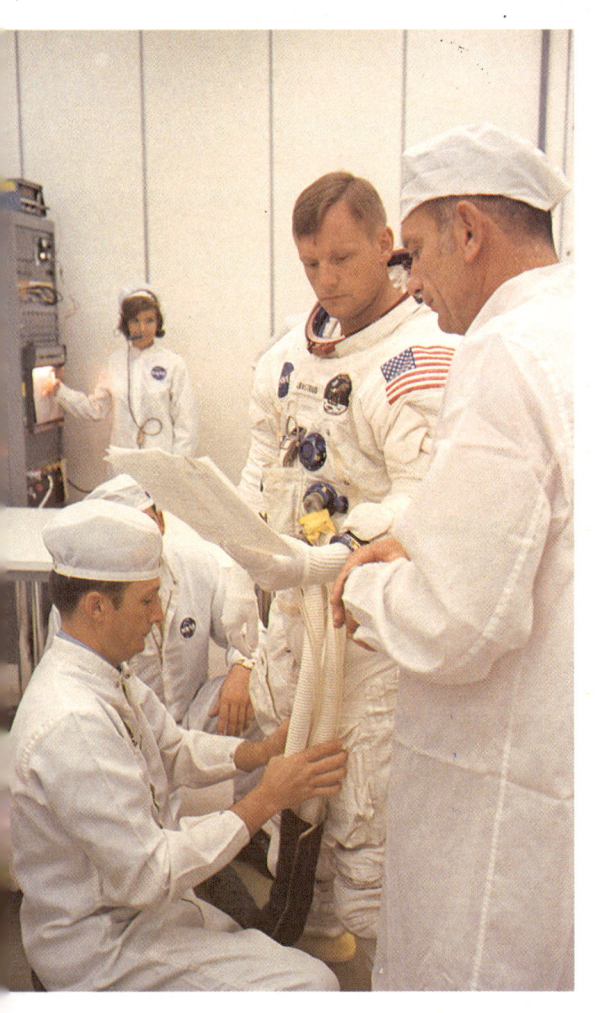

weighed almost 16 kg (35 lb). Though the suit may have appeared bulky and difficult to move in, it was in fact easy for the astronauts to move around or even kneel down because the waist, elbow and knee joints could be bent like an accordian. When not in their spacesuits, the crew could wear more comfortable overalls.

The first Apollo moon explorers, Armstrong and Aldrin, had to wear extra equipment for their moonwalks. First they replaced the "long johns" with underwear cooled by a network of plastic tubing filled with water. The astronaut's backpack or PLSS (Portable Life Support System) supplied the cooling water for the undergarment, and oxygen to breathe. The astronaut's breath was taken back into the PLSS to be cleaned. On top of the PLSS was a communications aerial and a system that could provide 30 minutes' emergency air supply.

The helmet had a plastic shell, and two visors with coatings to protect them against impact, tiny meteorites, heat and exposure to ultraviolet and infra-red radiation. Special gloves were also provided. These had an outer shell of special fabric and thermal insulation to protect the astronauts when handling extremely hot or cold objects. The extra-sensitive fingertips were made of silicon rubber. The special spacesuit worn by the astronauts for their moonwalks weighed 83 kg (183 lb) including PLSS backpack.

The Launch

The flight of Apollo 11 was such an amazing prospect that it made headlines long before the launch. By launch day, July 16, 1969, the excitement was easy to see. Nearly 3,000 press, radio and TV reporters from all over the world assembled at the press site at the Kennedy Space Center, about 5 km (3 mi) from the launch pad. Thousands of people were watching from other vantage points all around the Kennedy Space Center and Cape Canaveral, and millions were watching on TV or listening to radios. The launch was still hours away!

After eating the traditional pre-flight breakfast and putting on their spacesuits, the three astronauts emerged from the Manned Spacecraft Operations Building to be taken by van to the launch pad. Hundreds of cameramen took their photographs while the crowd shouted and cheered good luck to the crew, who waved back.

The van arrived at pad 39A. The astronauts got out and looked up at the towering white rocket that would soon be taking them into space. An elevator took them up the launch tower. They crossed a walkway to enter the small "clean room"; the hole in its wall was the open door of the command module. Armstrong took off his outer boots and got in first. Collins followed and Aldrin took the center of the three chairs.

Above *The control room at the space center was buzzing with excitement.*

Below *Before the launch the astronauts ate a large breakfast together.*

The launch of Apollo 11 was an amazing sight. Clouds of steam and flames surrounded it, and the takeoff could be seen for miles around.

From the press site, the Saturn rocket looked about as high as a matchstick held at arm's length. It stood there in the haze of a Florida summer morning, and, as the countdown neared zero, silence fell over the crowd, and all eyes were fixed on the launch pad. A loudspeaker blared the words, "Twelve, eleven, ten, nine, ignition sequence start." A huge ball of reddish-orange flame appeared at the base of the Saturn. "Six, five, four." Huge clouds of steam were produced as thousands of gallons of water cooled the launch pad. "All engines running, three, two, one, zero, liftoff. We have liftoff, thirty-two minutes past the hour. Liftoff on Apollo 11. Tower cleared."

Cheers and screams of joy were heard all around. People clapped, and some even wept. Saturn climbed away silently because the sound of its engines had not yet reached the press site. Then, as the rocket began to roll gently into its correct flight path, the noise arrived. The ground shook at the deafening roar created by the launch. The sky was so clear that Saturn could be seen until it was a speck in the sky and a gentle murmur in the distance. On the ground the experience was over. But in the command module, it was just beginning.

The crew was quiet during the launch and only made short reports. Then at T plus 11 minutes 40 seconds, the single engine of the S4B stopped. "Shutdown," said Armstrong. They were in orbit.

From the Earth to the Moon

Still attached to the S4B stage, Apollo flew around the earth one and half times while the crew checked all the systems. Then, at T plus 2 hours 44 minutes, 15 seconds over the Pacific Ocean, the engine of the S4B fired again. This was the start of the Trans-Lunar Injection, or TLI. The astronauts were suddenly pressed into their seats by the force of the acceleration. Apollo had achieved "escape velocity," which meant it was traveling fast enough to escape the pull of the earth's gravity. "Hey, Houston," said a pleased Armstrong, "that Saturn gave us a magnificent ride."

The crew now had to prepare for the transposition and docking maneuver (this was called T and DM by NASA). The command module had to separate from the S4B, turn around and dock with the top of the lunar module, which was still inside the third stage. Mike Collins moved to the center seat and carried out the transposition movements. He docked with the lunar module about 6 minutes later, and pulled the lunar module away from the S4B. The parts of Apollo that remained were the command and service module, *Columbia*, and the lunar module, *Eagle*. The astronauts were about 5,000 km (3,000 mi) from earth, gliding toward the moon.

The time during the flight toward the moon was spent in checking the lunar module, *Eagle*. Armstrong and Aldrin opened the hatch between the

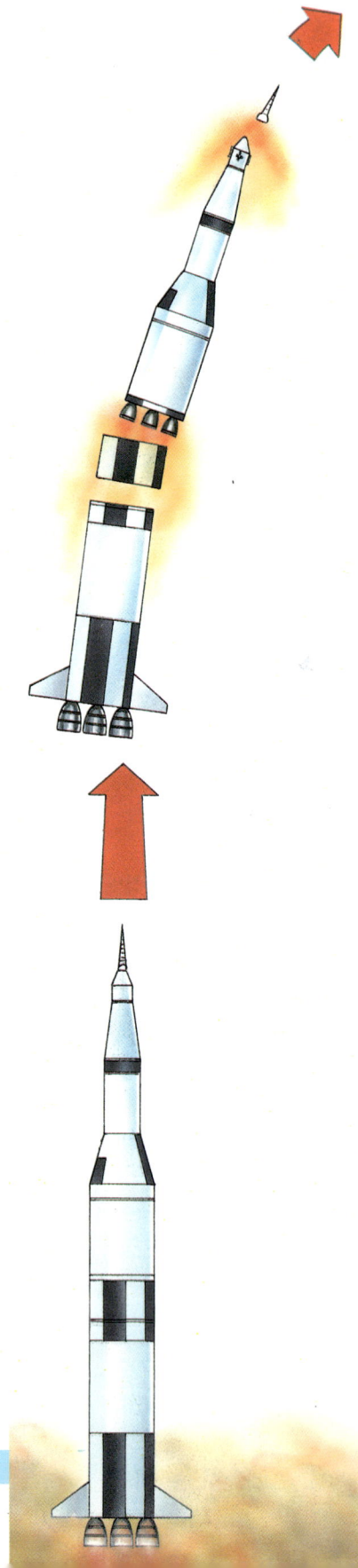

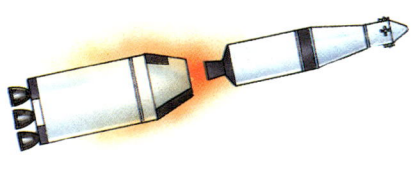

Left, above and right
These illustrations show how the different sections of Apollo 11 were abandoned after takeoff. In space, the command module turned around and docked with the lunar module, which had been stored in the last remaining section of the Saturn 5 rocket. Armstrong and Aldrin then floated into the lunar module to prepare it for its landing on the moon.

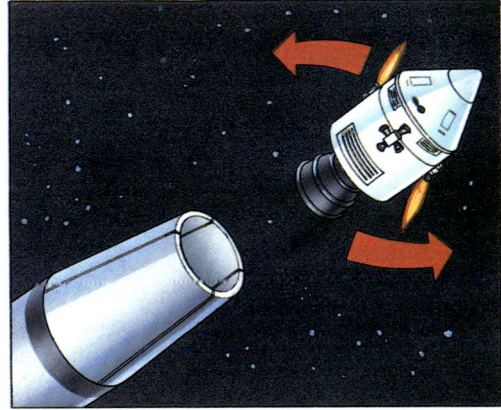

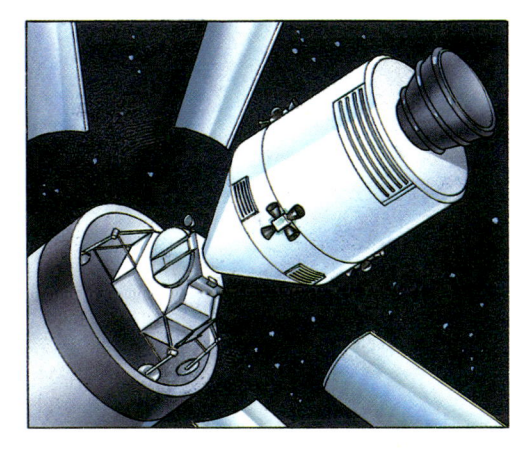

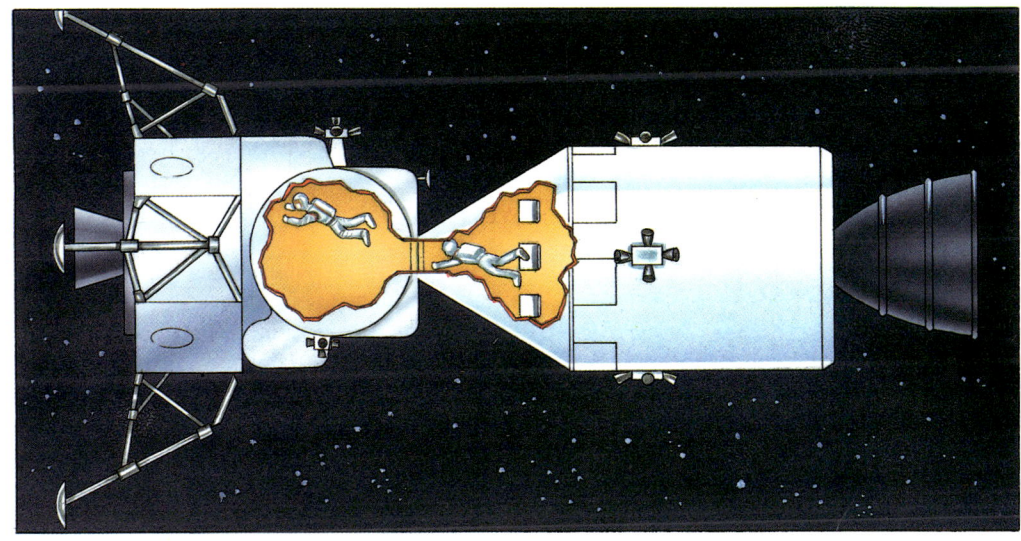

Far left *This is one of the first television pictures to be broadcast from space during the Apollo 11 mission. Although the image is blurred, it is easy to recognize the figure. It is the commander, Neil Armstrong.*

two craft and floated into *Eagle* to prepare it for its flight to the surface of the moon.

The flight path needed to be corrected slightly by firing the service module's engine. This was called a mid-course maneuver. The flight path was called a free return trajectory. This meant that if a landing was not possible, the craft would loop the moon and head back to earth, without the need for any major engine firings. (Later Apollo crews were not given this safety feature.) Apollo gradually slowed down as the earth's gravity tried to pull it backward, but then, as it entered the influence of the moon's gravity, the craft accelerated again.

Meanwhile, millions of people followed the flight eagerly. The mission was headline news and the subject of special television shows. The astronauts themselves were featured in some of them, in live pictures beamed from the command module. This gave the viewers the feeling that they were participating in the mission. For a few days, the world was united in following the progress of the American astronauts.

Apollo 11 plunged toward the moon, now only 130 km (80 mi) away. It was time for LOI, or Lunar Orbit Insertion.

Eagle Lands on the Moon

The Lunar Orbit Insertion was a very worrying time. The engine firing took place as Apollo 11 was moving around the far side of the moon and was out of contact with the earth. "Everything looks OK," said Armstrong before radio contact was lost. About seven minutes later the engine of the service module fired. This was to slow Apollo down so that it would enter lunar orbit from 95 to 270 km (59-167 mi) from the surface of the moon. Had it fired? The world wanted to know. Ground control in Houston, Texas, sent a message to Apollo. "Reading you loud and clear," replied Collins. Apollo 11 had made it.

Armstrong and Aldrin went into the lunar module, *Eagle*. Apollo 11 went behind the moon once more, and Armstrong separated *Eagle* from *Columbia*. As it came around the moon again and radio contact was restored, he said "The *Eagle* has wings." Again the two spacecraft went behind the moon. Now *Eagle's* descent engine fired, lowering the height of its orbit to only 15,000 m (49,000 ft). This was called the Descent Transfer Orbit.

Next came the Powered Descent Initiation, or PDI, that would slow *Eagle* down, and bring it in to land. Communications were getting very bad and ground control was worried. "If you can hear, you are go for PDI," said capsule communicator Charlie Duke, who was an astronaut himself. The engine lit up and fired continuously for 756 seconds.

The communication problems continued. At last, Duke said, "OK, we got you now." When *Eagle* was 2 minutes 11 seconds into the PDI and at an orbit of 14,000 m (46,000 ft), an alarm flashed in the cockpit. The computer was being overloaded with commands. "You are go," said Duke, and then repeated the message. At about 2,000 m (6,500 ft) *Eagle* pitched over so the crew could see the moon through the window. Another alarm flashed. Armstrong asked if he was still cleared for landing. "Give me a reading on the program alarm," he shouted.

Things were not looking good. A young computer engineer named Steve Bales saved the Apollo 11 mission. He checked the information and told Duke that everything was "go." It was a brave decision. Duke shouted, "You are go, you are go." Time and fuel were running out. As the surface approached, there was another computer alarm. "12:01 alarm," said Aldrin. Duke shouted, "Hang tight, you're go!" At 430 m (1,400 ft), Armstrong noticed that *Eagle* was heading toward a huge crater strewn with rocks. While Armstrong looked out of the window, Aldrin read him the information he needed to know about their speed and height.

Above *This photograph was taken from the command module and shows the lunar module ascent stage on its journey back from the surface of the moon.*

About 30 m (98 ft) above the surface, only a minute's worth of fuel remained. Aldrin's words were heard all over the world. "Picking up some dust, faint shadows, drifting to the right a little." Duke shouted, "30 seconds!" "Drifting right," said Aldrin, "Contact light!" Armstrong waited for a second and switched off the engine.

It was July 20, 1969; men had landed for the first time on the moon. There was silence. Then Armstrong quietly said, "Houston, Tranquillity Base here. The *Eagle* has landed." Duke replied. "Roger Tranquillity, we copy you on the ground. You've got a bunch of guys about to turn blue. We're breathing again. Thanks a lot."

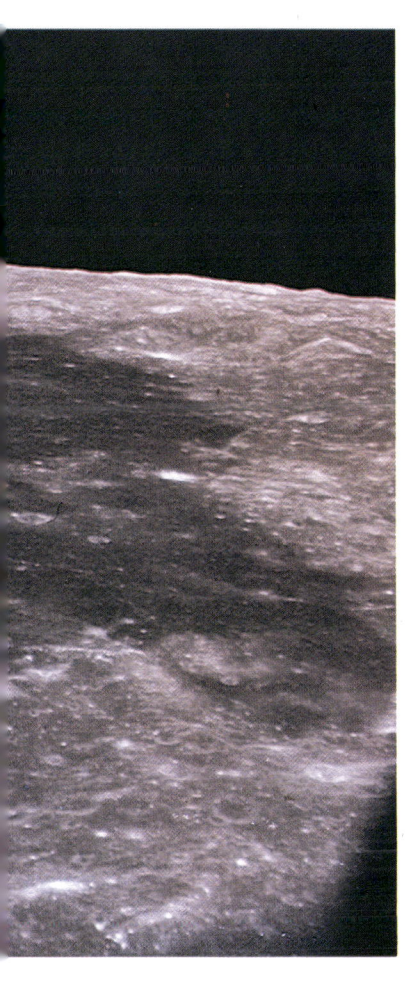

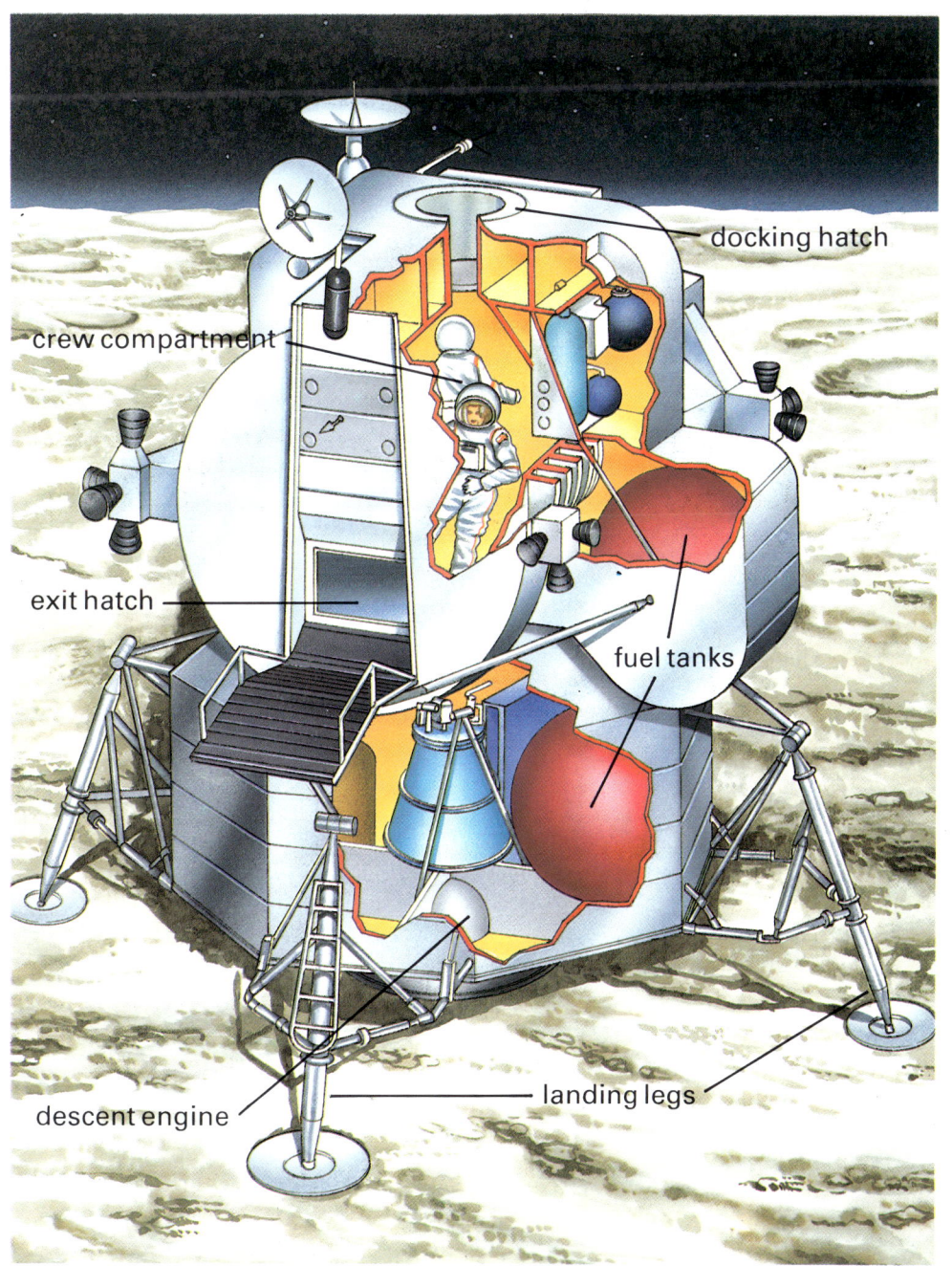

Right *Most of the space inside the lunar module was taken up by huge fuel tanks, so the astronauts did not have much room to move around. This illustration has been cut away to show the interior of the lunar module.*

21

Walking on the Moon

According to the Apollo 11 flight plan Armstrong and Aldrin were supposed to sleep after their landing on the moon. Not surprisingly, both astronauts felt so excited that they could not sleep. They decided to prepare for their moon walk earlier than planned. Even so it took four hours to get ready. At last, all was ready and the astronauts opened the hatch.

Armstrong lay face down with his feet at the open door and crawled backward onto the porch at the top of the ladder leading down one of the four landing legs. He slowly moved down the ladder and turned on a TV camera fixed to it. Ghostly black and white pictures appeared on TV screens at home, but at first, Armstrong appeared to be upside down! The TV fault was quickly corrected.

Armstrong jumped down from the last rung of the ladder onto the landing leg's footpad. "I'm going to step off the LM now," said Armstrong (LM means lunar module). He placed his left boot onto the surface of the moon and spoke the now-famous words, "That's one small step for man, one giant leap for mankind." The time was 9:56 p.m., Houston time on July 21, 1969.

Then Aldrin stepped onto the moon and described the stark, barren and flat surface, bathed in bright sunlight against a black sky. "Magnificent desolation," he said. The two men uncovered a plaque fixed

Above *Aldrin and Armstrong had to climb down a ladder to get to the surface of the moon.*

Above *The flag the astronauts left on the moon had to be stiffened with wire because there was no wind to make it flutter.*

Left *Aldrin and Armstrong placed many pieces of scientific equipment on the lunar surface. These would help scientists on earth discover more about the moon.*

to one of the landing legs. Armstrong read out the words on the plaque. "Here men from the planet earth first set foot upon the moon. We came in peace for all mankind."

The astronauts set up the United States' Stars and Stripes (stiffened with wire as there was no air on the moon to make it flutter). President Richard M. Nixon spoke to the astronauts on the moon by telephone from the White House in Washington.

By now the scientists on the ground were getting impatient because they felt that not enough actual exploration was being carried out. Armstrong and Aldrin put out scientific instruments on the moon's surface and collected rock samples. Aldrin tried a new way of moving about the surface, jumping along like a kangaroo! Two hours and 31 minutes after opening the hatch, the astronauts were back inside. With them were 35 kg (78 lb) of moon rocks.

Many pictures have been published of Aldrin standing on the moon. It is amazing that no one thought to ask Aldrin to take a photograph of Armstrong who was, after all, the mission's commander. But, apart from film taken automatically from the cockpit of the lunar module, only one picture exists of the first man on the moon. He is seen in shadow with his back to the camera!

Homeward Bound

The two astronauts slept badly after their moonwalk. It was cold, and the moon rocks had a smell rather like gunpowder. The two men were very excited about what they had done. After about 22 hours on the moon's surface at Tranquillity Base, it was time to take off for the rendezvous and docking with *Columbia*. On board the command module, circling the moon while waiting for his friends, was Mike Collins. Collins had been described in one newspaper as the "loneliest man in the universe" because sometimes during his lone orbits of the moon, he was out of touch with both ground control and the two moon explorers below.

Inside the ascent stage of *Eagle*, Armstrong and Aldrin made the final checks before what they hoped would be a successful ignition. The engine had to burn for 7 minutes 14 seconds. "You're cleared for takeoff," said capsule communicator Ron Evans, another astronaut. "Roger, understand," said Aldrin. "We're number one on the runway." He read out a countdown "six, five, abort stage, engine arm ascent, proceed." The engine fired. The ascent stage took off quickly. It moved upward in a straight line, its exhaust blowing over the flag left on the moon's surface. "That was beautiful," said Aldrin.

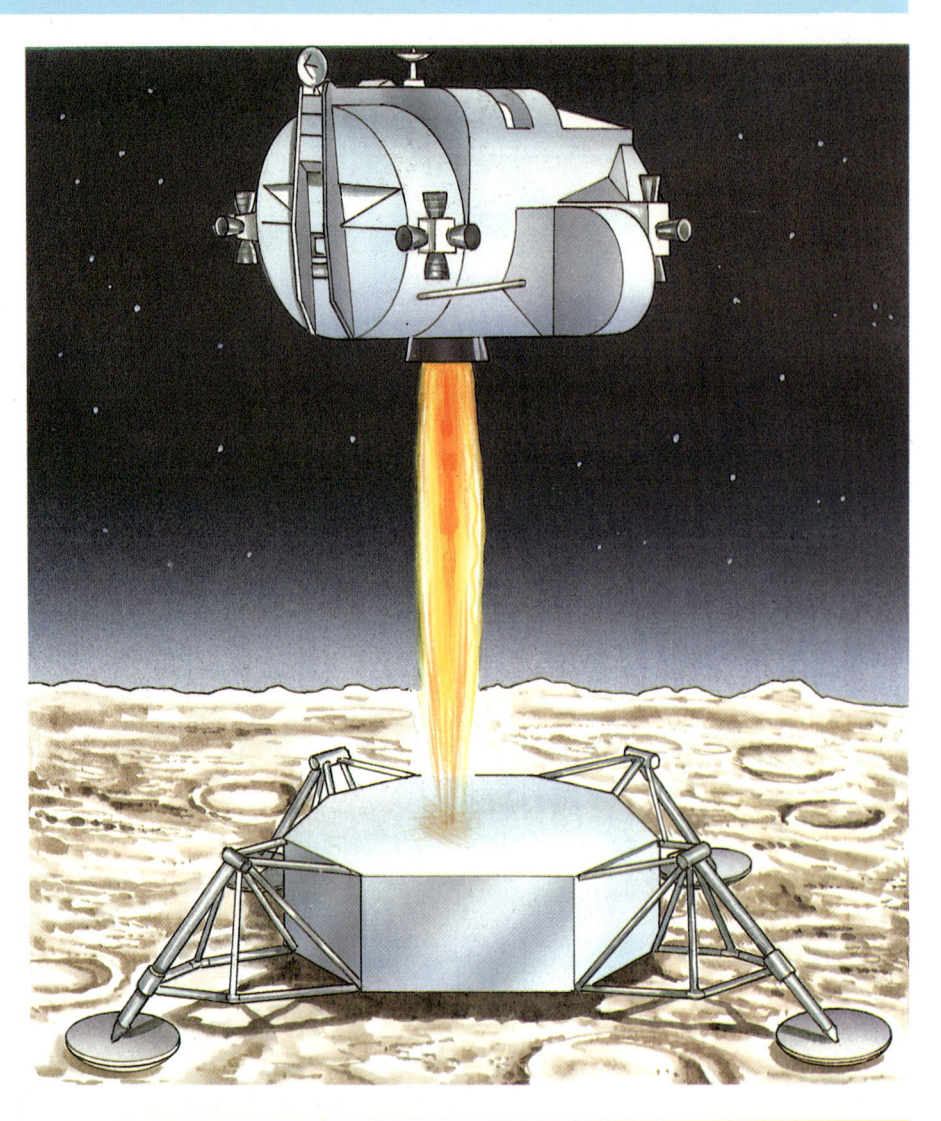

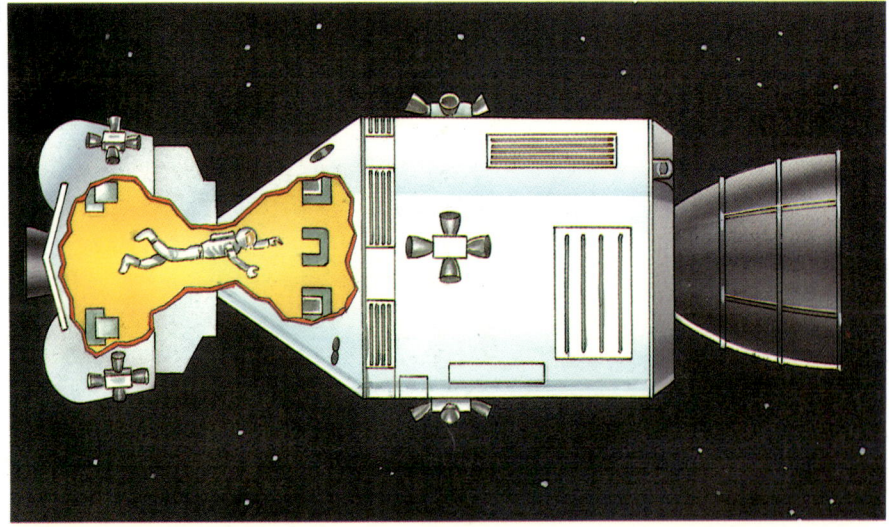

The engine worked perfectly and *Eagle* entered orbit. *Columbia* closed in for the docking. Viewers on the earth watched as a camera on *Columbia* recorded *Eagle's* approach. The docking was worrying to watch as the two craft appeared to jerk more than had been expected. Finally it was done, and the two astronauts entered *Columbia*, to be greeted by Collins. The three astronauts were back together again.

The next job was to get rid of the ascent stage of *Eagle*. It was left in orbit around the moon, where it remains to this day. *Columbia's* engine then had to be fired to perform the Trans-Earth Injection (TEI) so that it could break out of lunar orbit. The TEI was to take place behind the moon. As *Columbia* disappeared from sight, Duke in ground control called, "You are go for TEI." The first signals were received at Houston as *Columbia* reappeared from behind the far side of the moon.

Duke asked "How did it go?" Armstrong replied happily, "Tell them to open the LRL doors, Charlie!" The LRL was the Lunar Receiving Laboratory at the Houston ground control center, where the moon rocks would be analyzed on their return.

On the homeward journey, the Apollo 11 crew televised a program from inside the command module. "Good evening," said Armstrong, "this is the commander of Apollo 11. A hundred years ago, Jules Verne wrote a book about a voyage to the moon. His spaceship *Columbiad* took off from Florida and landed in the Pacific Ocean after completing a trip to the moon. It seems appropriate to us to share with you some of the reflections of the crew as the modern-day *Columbia* completes its rendezvous with the planet earth and same Pacific Ocean tomorrow!" Then Collins, Aldrin and Armstrong spoke about their tremendous voyage.

Above *The command module had to withstand incredibly high temperatures as it re-entered the earth's atmosphere.*

Below *The command module separated from the bulky service module, which was then abandoned.*

Above left *The ascent stage of the lunar module took off and left the abandoned descent stage on the moon's surface.*

Below left *After docking, the astronauts floated back into the command module from the lunar module ascent stage and were reunited with Collins.*

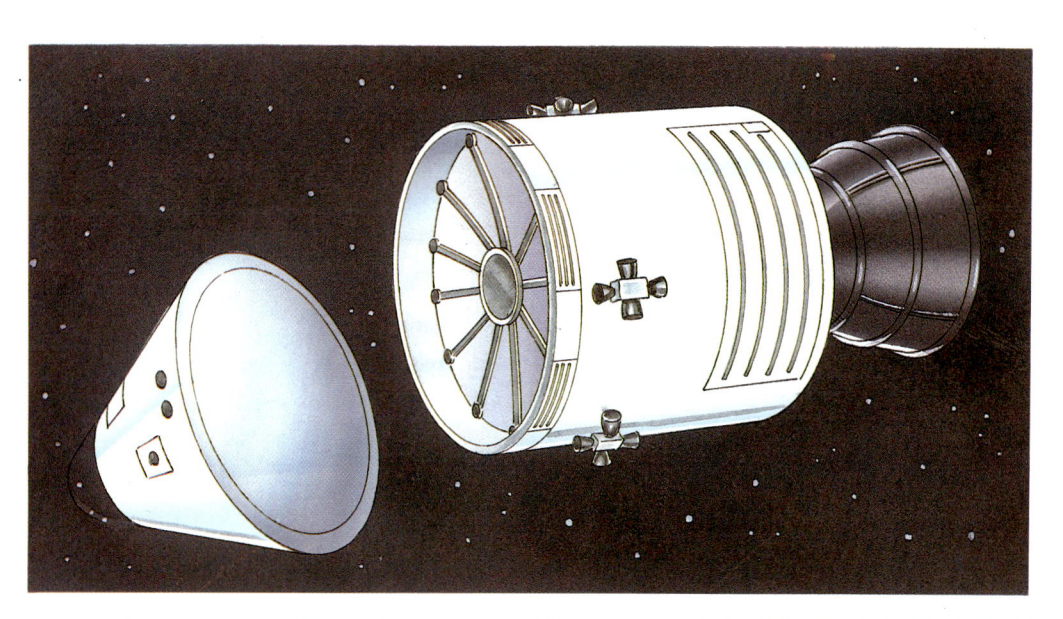

Splashdown

The reentry of the command module into the earth's atmosphere was a dangerous part of the Apollo 11 flight. Two previous Apollo missons (8 and 10) had achieved reentry successfully after flying around the moon, so it was not a completely unknown process. The main concern was that the module should enter the atmosphere at just the right angle, so that it would skip – like a flat stone bounced across water. This would slow the craft down and allow it to enter at the right speed and angle. The flight computer was performing correctly and everything looked good. Ten minutes before entry into the atmosphere, Apollo was traveling at about 27,000 kph (16,700 mph). The service module was detached and the cone-shaped command module was all that remained of the original Apollo spacecraft. Aldrin prepared the spacecraft for the final approach. "Gear is down and locked," he said. On board the recovery ship, the USS *Hornet*, which was sailing in the splashdown area in the Pacific Ocean, President Nixon waited to greet the astronauts.

Ten minutes later, the module made its first contact with the earth's atmosphere. "See you later," said Armstrong. Then radio communications from the astronauts were blacked out by the extremely high temperatures of reentry. The module flew perfectly through the atmosphere but the astronauts were subjected to a

Right *Much of the special resin that was used to protect the module from the heat of reentry had been burned away. The astronauts were picked up by divers and taken to the recovery ship.*

Left *The speed of the command module's descent was slowed down by several parachutes, which had been stored in its tip. The module floated down to a soft landing in the ocean.*

force of about six gs, six times the gravity on the earth's surface. Soon a small "drag chute," or parachute, was released to steady the module. This was followed by three other small parachutes, which in turn pulled out three enormous red and white striped landing parachutes. They were brightly colored to make them easy for the recovery crew to spot. Apollo hit the water and promptly turned upside down. This was no great problem because it had been planned for in advance; three balloons were released from the module's nose and pulled the spaceship upright.

Divers from the recovery ship soon reached the craft, and opened the hatch. The divers passed strange uniforms known as biological isolation garments to the three astronauts. The first explorers of the moon were to enter a special container on the recovery ship and stay in it without any physical contact with other people for three weeks. This was to make sure that they did not bring back unknown germs from the moon. At last the astronauts wearing their new isolation suits clambered into a raft and were soon in a helicopter flying to the USS *Hornet*, where they walked straight into the isolation container. Later they were seen at a window wearing normal clothes. President Nixon greeted the astronauts by intercom and called their mission "the greatest event since the creation."

The world went wild at the safe return of Apollo 11 after its voyage. The special isolation container, with the astronauts and moon rocks inside, was flown to Texas and arrived at the Lunar Receiving Laboratory of the Houston Space Center a few days later. By the time the astronauts left the container, the excitement was over. The moon rocks were cut into small pieces to be sent to laboratories all over the world for analysis. From these rock samples scientists learned a great deal about the moon, but many questions are still unanswered.

Above President Nixon came to see the three astronauts in their isolation container.

Below On the recovery ship the astronauts went into an isolation container where they would remain for three weeks. They wore suits to protect others from the germs they might have brought back.

The Legacy of Apollo 11

Apollo 11 had certainly achieved President Kennedy's aims. The United States now led the way in space exploration, and the USSR had been left well behind. Now, the sky – or rather space – was the limit! A Space Station . . . Space Shuttle . . . manned flights to the planet Mars. All these were to have been achieved within the next twenty years. But things did not happen as planned. The enormous advances created by Apollo 11 were not followed up, and today, the American space program has been overtaken by the USSR.

Apollo 13 failed to land on the moon, so just 12 people had walked upon the lunar surface when astronaut Eugene Cernan left the final footprints in December 1972. Because of cuts in the space budget, there were no moon landings after Apollo 17. No one has gone to the moon since then; there probably will not be another landing until the next century.

NASA was left with pieces of Apollo equipment, which were used in a space station project called Skylab. There were four Skylab missions, the last in 1974. A larger space station project was canceled, and NASA developed its revolutionary Space Shuttle on a much smaller budget. It should have been expected that NASA would have problems. The Shuttle (the world's first reusable spacecraft) took off four years late. Although it performed miracles in space, it was developed without enough money, and too much was expected of it. The *Challenger* disaster of 1986 was in a sense unavoidable. The Shuttle program will never be the same again, and flights to Mars remain only dreams.

Above *The space shuttle is the world's first reusable spacecraft. Until a shuttle exploded in 1986, this craft was thought to be the answer to many of the problems of space travel.*

And what happened to the astronauts of Apollo 11? Neil Armstrong, who was shy and quiet, never attempted to take advantage of his fame. He rarely talked publicly about the moon landing. He became a university professor and later he was the chairman of a computer company. He served on several presidential commissions on space, and as vice-chairman of the inquiry into the 1986 Shuttle disaster. He lives quietly on his farm in Ohio and avoids any publicity.

Michael Collins wrote the best book about the astronaut program and the flight of Apollo 11. It was called *Carrying the Fire*. His charming personality is demonstrated throughout the book. After the Apollo mission Collins took a number of government jobs and for a time was a business executive.

For Buzz Aldrin things never went well from the moment he came back from space. Aldrin had been a great achiever all his life. Apollo 11 was the height of his many achievements, and afterward there was nowhere to go but down. Unable to come to terms with life after the moon adventure, Aldrin had a breakdown, he became an alcoholic and suffered two broken marriages. He recovered and is now a professor at the University of North Dakota.

The Apollo project happened because of a combination of world events: the hostile political atmosphere between the USSR and the United States during the 1950s; the rapidly developing space technology of the 1960s that captured the imagination of the world; and a youthful American President, eager to increase his country's prestige throughout the world.

Left *The crew of Apollo 11 went on a world tour to give talks about their amazing journey. Neil Armstrong is seen here, with the other team members around him, talking to Congress.*

Glossary

Apollo project The United States space program for putting men on the moon.

Astronaut One who travels into space.

Centrifuge A machine that simulates the acceleration and deceleration felt by astronauts during spaceflight.

Command module The section of the spacecraft containing the control panel and quarters for the crew.

Cosmonaut The Soviet term for astronaut.

Countdown Minute-by-minute and second-by-second preparation for the liftoff at the start of a spaceflight, reentry or other maneuver.

Desolation An area or condition that is remote, barren or lonely.

Docking Joining of two spacecraft in space.

EVA Extra Vehicular Activity–walking in space or on the moon.

Excrete To pass out waste products from the body.

Feces Waste matter passed out from the body in solid form.

Fuel One of the two propellants used in a rocket. The other is the oxidizer.

Gemini project The United States space program designed to test the skills needed for landing on the moon.

Heatshield The covering on a spacecraft designed to protect it from the high temperatures created by reentering the earth's atmosphere.

Ignition The firing or lighting of engines or fuel.

LOI Lunar Orbit Insertion, when a spacecraft enters the moon's orbit.

Lunar Relating to the moon.

Lunar module The section of the spacecraft used to carry astronauts to the surface of the moon and back.

Mercury project The United States space program to put astronauts into orbit around the earth.

NASA National Aeronautics and Space Administration. The United States agency responsible for space programs.

Navigation Steering or plotting a route for a journey.

Orbit The path of a spacecraft or other object that continually goes around the earth, the moon or any other planetary body.

Oxidizer One of the two propellants of a rocket. The oxidizer helps to burn the other propellant, which is the fuel.

PDI Power Descent Initiation, a rocket firing during a landing on the moon.

PLSS Portable Life Support System used by astronauts while walking on the moon or in space.

Propellants The fuel and oxidizer used by rockets.

Reentry The return of a spacecraft to the earth's atmosphere on its journey back from space.

Rendezvous The meeting of two or more spacecraft in space.

Satellite An object that orbits another body such as the earth or the moon.

Saturn 5 The rocket that launched Apollo II to the moon.

Service module The section of the spacecraft containing an engine, the fuel tanks, air, water and power supplies.

Simulators Machines in which astronauts practice for their spaceflights. They copy the conditions that the astronauts will find in space.

Sputnik The first earth satellite launched by the USSR.

Statistics Information presented in the form of figures, charts or graphs.

TEI Trans-Earth Injection, the flight from the moon back to the earth.

TLI Trans-Lunar Injection, the flight from earth to the moon.

Urine Liquid produced by the kidneys and passed from the body as a waste product.

Vanguard TV-3 The United States satellite that was destroyed in an explosion in December 1957.

Finding out More

You can find out more by contacting the following:

NASA
Washington, D.C.
600 Independance Avenue
South West
Washington, D.C.
20546

John F. Kennedy Space Center
Florida
32899

Books to Read

Your local library should be able to help you find these books.

Norman Barrett, *Astronauts* Franklin Watts, 1986
Stewart Cowley, *Space Flight* Warwick Press, 1982
Chris Crocker, *Great American Astronauts* Franklin Watts, 1988
Tim Furniss, *Let's Look at Outer Space* Franklin Watts, 1987
Tim Furniss, *Our Future in Space* Bookwright Press, 1985
Tim Furniss, *Space* Franklin Watts, 1985
Tim Furniss, *Space Rocket* Gloucester Press, 1988
Christopher Lampton, *Rocketry* Franklin Watts, 1988
Graham Rickard, *Spacecraft* Bookwright Press, 1987
Gregory Vogt, *Space Ships* Franklin Watts, 1988
Gregory Vogt, *Space Stations* Franklin Watts, 1988
Gregory Vogt, *A Twenty Fifth Anniversary Album of NASA* Franklin Watts, 1983

Picture acknowledgments

The photographs in this book were provided by: Barnaby's Picture Library 6, 10, 14 (bottom left and bottom right), 16 (bottom), 25, 27 (top left, top right and bottom); Bruce Coleman Ltd 12; PHOTRI *frontispiece*, 18, 20, 22 (top and bottom), 23; Science Photo Library 5, 7, 16 (top), 29; Topham Picture Library 7; ZEFA Picture Library 4, 28, 17. Artwork by Peter Bull.

Index

Apollo 8 **7, 26**
Apollo 10 **26**
Apollo 11
  the astronauts **6–7**
  booster rocket **10–11**
  flight back to earth **24–5**
  flight to moon **18–19**
  launching of **16–17**
  moon landing **20–21**
  moonwalk **22–3**
  the spacecraft **12–13**
  spacesuits for **14–15**
  splashdown **26–7**
  training **8–9**
Apollo 13 **28**
Apollo 17 **28**
Apollo program **5, 6, 30**
ascent stage **5, 13, 24–5**
astronauts
  characteristics of **7**
  selection of **6**
  training of **8–9**

Cape Canaveral **16**
Cernan, Eugene **28**
Challenger **28, 29**
Columbia **18, 20, 24–5**
command module **5, 12, 18, 24, 26**

descent stage **5, 13**

Eagle **18–19, 20–21, 24–5**
Energia booster rocket **10**

food, in space **8**

Gargarin, Yuri **5**
Gemini program **7, 30**
Germany
  V2 rocket **4**

heatshields **5, 12, 30**
Hornet, USS **26–7**
Houston Space Center **20–21, 25, 27**

isolation container **27**

Kennedy, President John F. **5, 28, 30**
Kennedy Space Center **10, 16**

liftoff **10, 17**
lunar module **5, 12–13, 18**
lunar orbit **7, 12, 20, 25**
Lunar Receiving Laboratory **25, 27**

Mercury program **5, 30**
moon landing **20–21**
  commitment to **5**
moon rocks **23, 24, 25, 27**
moonwalk **22–3**

National Aeronautics and Space Administration (NASA) **7, 28**
Nixon, President Richard M. **23, 26, 27, 28**

Portable Life Support System **15**

rockets, development of **4, 5**

satellites **4–5, 30**
Saturn 5 rocket **5, 10–11, 12–13, 30**
service module **5, 12, 18–19, 26**
simulations **8, 30**
Skylab **28**
Space Shuttle **28–9**
spacesuits **9, 14–15**
splashdown **26–7**
Sputnik 1 **5, 30**

Tranquillity Base **21, 24**
Trans-Earth Injection **25, 30**
Trans-Lunar Injection **18, 30**

United States
  flag and plaque on moon **23**
  space race **4–5, 28–9**
USSR
  space race **4–5, 28–9**

Vanguard TV-3 **4, 30**

weightlessness **8**
World War II
  V2 rocket developed **4**